CLAUDE MONET

HOW THE FATHER OF IMPRESSIONISM TRANSFORMED FRENCH PAINTING

LEOTA C RAY

Copyright © 2024 by Leota C. Ray

All rights reserved. No part of this book may be used or reproduced in any form whatsoever without written permission except in the case of brief quotations in critical articles or reviews.

Printed in the United States of America.

CONTENTS

1 CHAPTER ONE: THE STRUGGLE FOR LIGHT AND INNOVATION..................4

2 CHAPTER TWO: MONET'S EMOTIONAL LANDSCAPE................................18

3 CHAPTER THREE: THE COLOR REVOLUTION..35

Chapter One

The Struggle for Light and Innovation

Claude Monet was a little kid who lived in the late 18th and early 19th centuries in the historic French port city of Le Havre on the coast of Normandy. At the time, nobody could have predicted that this little child would go on to become a legendary artist. The revolutionary new way of painting that Monet pioneered and popularized throughout his long and distinguished career came to be known as Impressionism. It was not an easy road to success, however. Because he was so committed to his craft, Monet lived in poverty for many years into his middle age. His fame, fortune, and the acclaim that resulted from his works as masterpieces did not come until much later in life. His paintings continue to fetch millions of dollars today, solidifying Monet's position as the most renowned Impressionist.

November 14, 1840 was the birthdate of Oscar Claude Monet in Paris. But his family relocated to Le Havre when he was five years old, and his father, Adolphe, became a prosperous grocer and ship's chandler there. Little is known about Monet's early life, and his school years didn't seem to be anything out of the ordinary. His creative skill, however, started to show itself when he was a teenager. Monet began selling his drawings and caricatures at a neighborhood art store for twenty francs each when he was fifteen years old.

Local artist Eugène Boudin also had his paintings shown in

this store. Because Boudin loved painting in the fresh air, he convinced the young Monet to do the same. As a result of this, Monet developed an obsession with working in nature that he never let go of.

Afterwards, Monet would say that it was a life-changing event that showed him what painting was capable of becoming, like a veil had been removed from his sight. Embracing the spontaneity and truthfulness of painting what was there in front of him, he subsequently dedicated himself to painting outdoors.

Natural light, as seen in the outdoors, was of special interest to Monet. He devoted the most of his life to this. The relentless pursuit of reality by Monet stands out as one of his most outstanding traits. Instead of doing an outside sketch and then completing the painting in the studio, he thought that painting an item in its natural environment was the only way to get the essence of it, whether it was a tree, a person, or a façade. Painting from a distance, in Monet's view, prevented him from capturing the essence of the moment, thus he sought to get as near to the sight as possible.

Monet would later consider the importance of his outdoor painting sessions with Boudin, stating that it was the moment when he felt a weight lifted off his shoulders and that his calling was to be a painter. As a result of this epiphany, Monet told his family he wanted to be an artist when he was still a teenager. He embarked on his adventure in May of 1859, heading for Paris, the cultural epicentre of France.

The city's bohemian culture captivated the young Monet. In addition to studying at the Swiss Academy, an open studio for budding painters, he mingled with the creative community in bars and cafés and attended the major yearly art show at the

Salon. Camille Pissarro, another young artist who would go on to become an influential role in the Impressionist movement, was there when he met her.

On the other hand, Monet did not accomplish much during his initial stay in Paris. He freely admitted that he was careless with his time and squandered a lot of it. This could have played a role in his father's choice not to pay to have him released from the army in 1861. Algeria was a North African colony when Monet was ordered to serve in the cavalry. Nevertheless, he was sent back home to recuperate after catching typhoid.

In order to terminate his military duty, Monet's aunt Sophie Lecadre stepped in and paid three thousand francs. Her kindness enabled him to go back to his work, and Monet took advantage of the chance as she was the one relative who really believed in his creative aspirations. With the intention of making the most of his second opportunity, he went to Paris in November 1862, vowing to devote more time to his work.

His illustrious second tenure in Paris began at this point. Monet became a student of the great French academic artist Charles Gleyre. Studio painting in the manner of the Old Masters was the primary emphasis of this school, which drew inspiration from mythology and historical events.

French painting was heavily skewed toward the classical tradition when Monet arrived at Charles Gleyre's workshop. Its rigid norms became familiar to Monet in no time. Nature is great as a study element, but it provides no appeal, Gleyre told Monet as he was criticizing his realistic depiction of a human model. You see, style is king. Despite his disagreement with Gleyre's views, Monet persisted in his studies there, making the most of his time at the studio, even though he was only 22 years old.

The time Monet spent at Gleyre's workshop was fruitful, notwithstanding their philosophical disagreements on painting. He befriended other painters, such as Frédéric Bazille, and two of the Impressionist era's most prominent figures, Auguste Renoir and Alfred Sisley. Located in the Fontainebleau forest, not far from Paris, these young painters started working together in 1863. Here, under the direction of the illustrious Camille Corot, members of the Barbizon School of painting rebelled against academic convention by bringing their canvases outside, making the place historically important. Compared to the vast historical or mythical images that the Paris Salon preferred, their landscapes were more realistic and the subjects more commonplace.

Midway through the 1860s, Monet was working on landscapes in Fontainebleau, creating works like "The Road from

Chailly." Despite the lack of revolutionary spirit in these paintings, Monet's self-assurance was skyrocketing, verging on hubris. Despite his severe poverty, Monet put on an air of aristocracy, even though he was not yet a well-known painter. He had an unfaltering faith in his abilities despite often pleading with Bazille and others for supplies and funds to paint.

When Monet began his first major piece in 1866, his strong feeling of self was at its peak. After seeing Édouard Manet's notorious "Le Déjeuner sur l'herbe," which had startled Parisian society three years before with its daring brushwork and portrayal of nudity in a modern park setting, Monet aspired to outdo Manet. In the 1866 Salon, the official yearly exhibition that was the ticket to success for every aspiring artist, he aimed to make a painting four times bigger than Manet's in the hopes that it would be a success.

Nevertheless, the scope of Monet's undertaking was too expansive. He was never able to finish the work because of its enormous size and his financial difficulties. Still, he reached a turning point in his career with that daring endeavor, showing that he was ready to question artistic standards and forge his own way forward.

Being bedridden due to a leg injury cost Monet precious time. He tried to continue his ambitious painting after a little recuperation, but he quickly realized he wouldn't be able to finish it in time for the Salon display. He also finished a number of drawings and a final oil study. Monet accepted this and then left the project, leaving behind just two big sections of the artwork. Nobody knows how the Salon would have felt about the finished picture. In contrast to the lyrical undertones of Édouard Manet's "Le Déjeuner sur l'herbe," which had served as inspiration for Monet, this picture depicted a more practical setting and modern attire.

Monet's rendition, which occupied about half of the painting's upper half, aimed to situate the people organically within an outdoor environment by highlighting the trees and terrain. Figures bathed in dappled sunshine by Monet seemed more at one with their natural environment than those by Manet, whose arrangement was more contrived.

Despite this setback, Monet continued to paint and displayed a more traditional portrait of a woman in a green dress at the Salon in 1866. In addition to the female figures in Monet's previous, unfinished piece, the model for this painting was his lover Camille Doncieux. After receiving positive feedback for *The Woman in a Green Dress*, Monet swiftly put his displeasure with the abandoned project behind him.

After that, Monet turned his attention to *Women in the Garden*, another piece he had submitted to the Salon. On this occasion, he chose to complete the massive painting outside. The eight-foot-tall canvas was too much for Monet's studio, so he excavated a tunnel and set up a pulley system to control its height. The feminine figures were posed for one again by Camille.

The vibrant color contrasts of *Women in the Garden* stood out, especially when compared to the verdant garden grass and the women's clothes. Though the finished artwork was important, the process of creating it was far more so. Legend has it that French realist Gustave Courbet dropped into Monet's studio while he was working and discovered the artist doing nothing. As time went on, Courbet recognized that Monet was only patiently awaiting the ideal lighting conditions before painting the tree leaves. Paying close attention to how light changes over time would become a trademark of Monet's later work.

Another French artist, Gustave Courbet, failed to grasp Monet's fixation on achieving uniform illumination over a whole painting. If Monet wanted his people, trees, grass, and every other element in the picture to have the same lighting scheme, he insisted on painting them all in the same light. All of the pieces came together to form a whole because of this uniformity. Monet was becoming more obsessed with depicting the way the eye perceived rather than how the mind made sense of it.

Many of Monet's contemporaries were also interested in optics and vision, therefore his method was only one facet of a wider creative movement. Michel Eugène Chevreul's color ideas piqued the curiosity of prominent scientists like Monet and Camille Pissarro, who were working on their own color theories at the same time. So, after the 1860s, artists like Monet and Pissarro stopped using any colors other than the three main ones and their complimentary shades.

In his early works, Monet drew inspiration from Édouard Manet's use of flat, color regions illuminated by direct, front-facing light that emphasized forms and details. In Monet's early painting *Women in the Garden*, he used this approach to great effect, painting the people in brilliant color while the background, which includes trees and grass, is shown in a more impressionistic way. Monet was only starting to dabble with the methods that would come to characterize his work.

The 1867 Salon jury, however, did not like Monet's ideas and rejected his entry, dealing a heavy defeat to the artist. Monet lived in abject poverty in the late 1860s. Camille Doncieux added to Monet's financial woes in 1867 when she gave birth to their son, Jean, while they were still unmarried.

While Pierre-Auguste Renoir remained in Louveciennes with

his parents, the Monet family had moved to Bougival, close to Paris, by 1869. In order to alleviate Monet and Camille's extreme poverty, Renoir would take food from his mother and give it to them. In spite of all this, the Impressionist movement was born out of the summer of 1869, when Monet and Renoir collaborated creatively on paintings overlooking the La Grenouillère, a body of water.

CHAPTER TWO

Monet's Emotional Landscape

In the year 1869, the esteemed Impressionist artists Claude Monet and Pierre-Auguste Renoir demonstrated remarkable productivity at La Grenouillère. Among the two, Monet exhibited a greater willingness to embrace innovative techniques. His application of bold, discontinuous brushstrokes intentionally eschewed fine detail in works such as **Bathers at La Grenouillère**, showcasing his distinct artistic approach. Instead of portraying the scene's delicate nuances, the artists just painted blobs of water and people enjoying a swim. Similar to how one cannot notice every detail in the visual field in real life, Monet depicted what was observed at a glance in his paintings.

Grenouillère* and *Bathers, two paintings with rather simple titles, showed a daring new way of using color. Using mostly basic colors and their complementary hues, both Monet and Renoir transitioned to working with unmixed colors. They learned that colors may change depending on their environment, which was a revelation that was prompted by chemist Eugène Chevreul's thoughts on color. They rethought how they painted shadows after this realization. While most artists used brown or black to portray shadows, Renoir and Monet started to shade them based on the colors around them. As a result of this finding, hitherto unseen artworks were created.

Shadows weren't only black, as Monet and Pissarro discovered together. Black was no longer an option in his color pallet by the 1860s. In fact, his shadows mirrored contrasting hues rather than being completely dark. A blue shadow, for example, may incorporate a subtle hint of orange to illustrate how shadows, much like ordinary objects, reflect the diverse colors present in their environment.

Monet's dedication to plein air painting allowed him to deeply observe the interplay of light and shadow on various hues, revealing his growing fascination with luminance. He meticulously documented every hue as it presented itself, unbound by traditional conventions. As a result, the shadows on his canvases exhibited an unprecedented degree of vibrancy and intensity, paralleling the brightness of the surrounding colors.

This innovative approach significantly transformed

perceptions of color. Monet's keen insight enabled him to elevate seemingly minor variations in light and shadow to an entirely new level of abstraction. While shadows have traditionally been viewed as the counterpart to light, often depicted in dark or black tones, Monet perceived them as possessing a richer complexity that deserved recognition. Objects not only absorbed and reflected light from their surroundings, but they also cast shadows when light is blocked in a certain direction. Thus, every shadow became distinct and endowed with its own essence.

Though groundbreaking creatively, these pieces achieved nothing to help Monet's persistent financial problems of the period.

The Luncheon, Monet's second effort at achieving Salon recognition in 1870, was a far more conservative work than his previous efforts at Bougival. However, following the rejection, he decided to discontinue his endeavors to exhibit at the Salon. Relieved of the expectations associated with the Salon during that summer, he returned to his personal artistic practices.

It was during this time in the Parisian studio of Charles Gleyre that Monet and Renoir initially encountered one another. The two painters probably wanted to make huge pieces, but they couldn't afford to. Consequently, artists started concentrating on creating smaller paintings, which was a turning point in the evolution of Impressionism. Their perspective shifted from seeing sketches as only preparatory work to seeing these smaller, more rapidly completed works as full-fledged paintings.

The Salon, which had previously insisted on massive, meticulously executed pieces, became alienated from them as a result of this change in technique. Nevertheless, it attracted a new kind of customer—those who were interested in buying smaller, more impressionistic works but couldn't afford the ten- to twelve-foot-tall big canvases.

On June 28 of that year, Monet entered into matrimony with Camille, despite facing ongoing financial difficulties. During their honeymoon in Trouville, Normandy, the couple, in a spirit of inspiration, saw Monet produce several miniature coastal landscapes. Evidence of their creation in a natural setting is notable in the sand particles integrated into the paint, as these pieces were executed entirely en plein air. **The Beach at Trouville** was an example of Monet's daring brushwork; the lady on the left, who happened to be his new wife, Madame Monet, exemplified this style. In alignment with Monet's evolving artistic vision, the importance of the depicted scene resides in the interpretation of the observer rather than solely in identifying the women portrayed in the artwork.

During that summer, Monet was accompanied by his colleague Eugène Boudin. His artistic development was evident as he created beach landscapes that differed markedly from those of his former mentor.

While at the beach, he captured an image of his wife amidst the backdrop of impending political turmoil, as the Franco-Prussian War began in July. Monet, holding anti-Empire sentiments, chose not to enlist and instead sought refuge in London with his wife and child, leaving Boudin to manage their affairs. This period proved crucial for Monet, as it allowed him the opportunity to study the works of Turner and Constable while continuing to create his own compositions.

A significant milestone in Monet's career was his encounter with art dealer Paul Durand-Ruel in London. The importance of Durand-Ruel's support for Monet and the Impressionist movement would prove to be substantial. Following the conclusion of the war in 1871, Monet returned to France where he quickly experienced an increase in purchasing power. With the assistance of the dealer who had acquired several of Monet's works, the artist and his family were able to establish residence in Argenteuil, a picturesque riverside area of Paris renowned for its boating resorts and regattas that attracted international competition.

Monet would find endless inspiration in the boats and river views of Argenteuil for the next seven years. **Boats, Regatta at Argenteuil**, a miniature he painted in 1872, is remarkable for the reflections it contains in the water and the speed with which it was done using unblended, self-contained colors. This painting, along with *The Red Boats* from 1875, exemplified Monet's skill with color as he emphasized the vitality of complimentary colors, such as green and red, in his works.

The innovative way Monet depicted water is what really made him famous. Historically, painters have approached water, sky, and trees as individual subjects, each calling for a unique approach. However, for Monet, there was a connection between everything. His perception of the water's hues was shaped by the environment around it. He was able to convey the essence of colors on canvas by studying their interactions. Each of his water-themed paintings was uniquely distinct, showcasing an exceptional talent for conveying motion and fluidity.

By constructing a mobile studio tethered to the riverbank, Monet was able to fully engage with the dynamic environment of the river, resulting in the creation of his celebrated plein air artworks. In 1874, Édouard Manet portrayed the esteemed artist Monet while he was exploring some of Monet's innovative techniques within this floating studio. The picture is well recognized today.

Artists such as Sisley and Renoir often paid Monet visits at Argenteuil during his stay there. As they worked side by side, they explored the emerging themes and concepts in their works.

These painters came up with a radical new concept in 1873: to have their own exhibition of paintings. Eleven painters, including Renoir, Monet, Sisley, Pissarro, and Degas, had assembled by December of that year to establish the Société Anonyme. Participating in a group display was their primary objective. Their works were initially shown to the public at the Parisian photographer Nadar's studios on April 15, 1874.

The prevailing perspectives regarding art educational institutions were significantly reexamined as a result of this exhibition. The featured artists opted for expressive color schemes and gestural brushwork, departing from conventional approaches that emphasize realistic representation and foundational elements such as perspective and outlines in traditional painting. Audience reactions included surprise and confusion at the display of what appeared to be an unfinished work by Monet, **Impression, Sunrise**, which was misconstrued as a reflection of ineptitude rather than a groundbreaking shift in artistic expression. Additionally, some critics perceived the reduction of human forms to mere color stripes as a point of contention and a source of offense.

In 1874, Monet presented twelve paintings at an exhibition, which faced significant criticism, particularly regarding their perceived lack of detail. The critic Louis Leroy famously remarked, "Wallpaper in its embryonic state is more finished than that seascape," thus vocalizing disapproval of Monet's artistic approach. This comment inadvertently led to the coining of the term **"Impressionism,"** which was later embraced by a new generation of artists keen to define their creative style. By the time of the eighth and final exhibition in 1886, "Impressionism" had become an established term; however, Monet did not partake in this final showcase, having participated in five of the preceding seven exhibitions.

In the second exhibition of 1876, Monet featured **The Japanese Girl**, with his wife serving as the model. This intriguing piece sold for 2,000 francs, indicating an attempt by its creator to capitalize on the contemporary fascination with Japanese prints. Notably, during the third exhibition in 1877, Monet presented a more extensive collection consisting of thirty paintings, seven of which depicted the Gare Saint-Lazare, a key railway terminus in Argenteuil, showcasing the same Parisian train station from various perspectives.

In January 1877, Monet executed a series of paintings focusing on the glass-roofed Gare Saint-Lazare station, characterized by its billowing steam and locomotives. Despite selling works such as *The Japanese Girl*, Monet faced financial challenges, exacerbated by the economic recession in France during the late 1870s. His art dealer, Paul Durand-Ruel, also struggled to purchase Monet's works amid this financial downturn.

Nevertheless, Monet adeptly maintained the appearance of affluence. He skillfully gained access to the Gare Saint-Lazare, orchestrating train stoppages and clearing platforms to fulfill his requirements as a prominent artist. This strategic behavior resulted in a series of audacious Impressionist paintings.

Throughout the 1870s, Monet returned to Paris to paint at the Gare Saint-Lazare, a site that particularly fascinated him due to its association with trains. In focusing on the effects of steam, he may have aimed to address critiques regarding the fog depicted in his London works. Noticing that steam could blur forms when illuminated by light, Monet sought to deepen his understanding of this meteorological phenomenon. His paintings effectively capture this effect, often rendering the structures behind the station nearly indistinguishable amidst patches of steam and sunlight.

Monet's exploration of the effects of fog spanned both urban and natural settings, with his interest in steam and artificial sources extending beyond this venue. While in London, he created a painting along the Thames River near Westminster that evocatively portrayed the city's atmosphere alongside its renowned fog.

He depicted the town of Vétheuil in 1879, expressing the melancholy he was encountering at the time via its chilly and subdued mood. It is hardly surprise that the picture has a somber tone, considering that Monet was mourning the death of his beloved wife, Camille, who died in September 1879 at the young age of 32. Since their second son, Michel, was born, Camille had been unwell.

At the time of Camille's passing, Monet's private life had transformed. Ernest and Alice Hoschedé were affluent Parisians whom he met in 1876. Following the financial challenges resulting from Ernest's bankruptcy and his subsequent departure from Alice and their five children—who had previously resided with Monet's family—Monet took on the responsibility of providing financial support for the third Impressionist exhibition. Subsequently, after the passing of his beloved Camille, Monet and Alice began collaborating closely, ultimately uniting in matrimony.

The loss of Camille marked a significant financial downturn for Monet. However, the early 1880s heralded an improvement in the French economy, which positively impacted Monet's financial situation. In 1881, esteemed art dealer Paul Durand-Ruel formalized a contractual agreement with Monet, ensuring him an annual income of thirty thousand francs. This period also signaled a transformation within the art world; traditional salons began to wane in influence as Durand-Ruel and others organized exhibitions focused on showcasing the works of individual artists. Despite facing ongoing criticism, the Impressionists' work gained increasing recognition and value.

In 1883, Monet relocated to Giverny, approximately 50 miles from Paris, with his two children. They joined Madame Hoschedé and her five children in residing at a property known as La Prise, or The Cider Press. Although the conventional rural community viewed Monet's nontraditional living arrangement with skepticism—particularly given his age of over 40—he prioritized his artistic pursuits. It took some time for him to shed the mindset of financial hardship; however, once he accomplished this, he experienced a newfound sense of security and comfort.

The 1880s marked a pivotal turning point in Monet's artistic journey as he began to manifest his creative vision. At Giverny, he once again utilized a floating studio to capture river scenes, effectively portraying the light and beauty of the surrounding countryside. His output during this period was exceptionally prolific.

CHAPTER THREE

THE COLOR REVOLUTION

Monet painted a breathtaking sequence of landscapes with humans in them, fully embracing his new environment. **Woman with a Parasol**, which he created in 1886, features Alice Hoschedé's daughter Suzanne, and is considered one of his most famous works. Instead than focusing on her face, Monet let the light and color do the talking in this painting. Choppy brushstrokes give the grass under her feet a feeling of motion and energy, highlighting the stark contrast between light and dark. The muted sky harmonizes with the delicate hues of the woman's garment, bringing the piece together to form one of Monet's most exquisite works.

Even though Monet had a soft spot for Giverny, he kept looking beyond the grounds for ideas. In 1886 he set out for Brittany, specifically to an isolated island known as Belle-Île that was exposed to the stormy Atlantic. Here he depicted the dramatic seascape *Storm Rocks at Belle-Île*, which was painted at the height of a storm. In his pursuit of realism, he took on the Normandy arched cliffs, particularly the world-renown Manneport. Unfazed by his near-drowning experience the year before, he resumed his exploration of this topic and successfully created an enduring picture of nature by navigating perilous trails.

By this point, Monet had embraced a novel approach: he

would paint the same subject on many canvases at once, each portraying it in slightly varied lighting. He thought that the light that danced between an item and the spectator was more important than the thing itself. As he attempted to capture the ever-changing effects of sunshine and clouds on his canvases, he was captivated by this otherworldly interaction.

For this, Monet devised a device that, like a rack, supported many identically sized canvases. He would paint on different canvases depending on the available light, resulting in unique works that had a same topic. He was able to delve into the subtleties of color and light in ways that had never been done before because to this method.

Monet was also experiencing a period of commercial success. He was about to embark on a new phase of his creative career as both his reputation and the worth of his works were rising.

He accomplished a great deal in "86" when he had his first exhibition in America. His work was on display at a big Paris exhibition with that of sculptor Rodin only three years later, in 1889. There was still a long way to go for Monet, who had already become a major player in the art world by the early 1890s.

A revolutionary body of work that would represent the zenith of Impressionism was unveiled by him in 1891. These series were based on a really simple idea: painting the same subject over and over again to see how different lighting affects the topic. Regardless of the weather, he began this effort with the *Haystack* series. Attempting to freeze a moment in time, Monet painted each canvas to depict a different light effect that engulfed the area.

Commercially and critically, the *Haystack* series was a smashing success, firmly establishing Monet as a leading figure in the art world. After this success, he shifted his focus to the *Poplars*, a series depicting the lofty trees that border the river Epte, close to his Giverny house. But when Monet found out that the trees were going to be cut down, the whole endeavor was about to go down the drain. Luckily, he was able to convince the lumber merchant to delay the cutting until he could finish his job.

After finishing the *Poplar* series, Monet began working on the *Rouen Cathedral* series, which he considered to be his masterpieces in the genre. In 1892 and 1893, he painted a spectacular series of thirty paintings, each depicting a different aspect of the magnificent Gothic cathedral's stone façade. Monet attempted to depict the passing of time by painting on as many as fourteen canvases simultaneously from as few as three distinct vantage points.

He captured the structure of the cathedral under changing

light conditions throughout the day by building up the picture with thick layers of paint. Again, Monet was able to capture the all-encompassing effects of light, revealing his command of this transient element and its powerful influence on perception. The church came to life as he painted it, taking in the surrounding light and weather with each brushstroke.

Light and shadow create a dynamic relationship in Monet's *Full Sunlight*, which brings the old stone of the cathedral to life. The sun's rays seem to melt the solid facade, casting lovely shadows inside the arches that give the whole thing a liveliness and otherworldliness. There is no mistaking the strong correlation between the weather and the feelings conveyed by this painting when seen in the context of the other works in the *Rouen Cathedral* series. It was an incredible achievement to accomplish this illusion with a building made of stone that seemed to be devoid of life.

Early in his career, Monet started painting on many canvases simultaneously; he perfected this technique in the 1870s and 1880s, especially with the *Rouen Cathedral* series. He was able to capture the cathedral in an impressive range of moods using this way. At times of intense sunshine, the cathedral's shapes seem to melt into shades of white and yellow, creating a breathtaking atmospheric shift.

The exhibition of twenty paintings from the *Cathedral* series in 1895 solidified Monet's position as a prominent artist. His star rose throughout France and beyond as each of his paintings fetched a staggering 15,000 francs at auction. After marrying Alice Hoshid in 1892 and securing his beloved property in Giverny two years earlier, Monet was 55 years old and had finally achieved personal satisfaction. He was also well renowned for his artistic abilities.

At Giverny, Monet devoted more and more of his energy to his garden, creating a verdant flowery haven. He hired six gardeners to help him create this paradise with his newfound fortune. He went to great lengths to get authorization to redirect the little River Ru, which he then used to create a verdant sanctuary in his garden. His most vibrant and vivid paintings were inspired by this magical landscape as he aged older.

However, Monet's need for creative inspiration via travel never was satisfied. He and Alice had a chauffeured early model vehicle on their 1904 journey to Spain. In 1908 and 1909, he also paid important trips to Venice. Still, a few years before, in 1899, 1900, and 1901, he embarked on his most formative creative adventures in London, where he sought fresh viewpoints to enhance his continuously developing corpus of work.

Over one hundred paintings depicting famous London sights

including Charing Cross, Waterloo Bridge, and the Houses of Parliament which were created by Monet when he stayed at the Savoy Hotel, which had a view of the Thames. Atmospherics, light, and color were the central concerns of his painting in these pieces, with the majestic Parliament buildings being just subtly hinted at.

Monet spent more and more time in his garden in his latter years. The Japanese bridge he had constructed over the lily pond served as the inspiration for several of his subsequent works, even though he had severe vision problems. Still, the same lily pond inspired him to create his magnum opus of art.

In 1898, Monet had imagined a chamber with a circular layout, encircled by canvases of tranquil lilies floating on an uninterrupted sea of water. After years of little development, Monet finally received a commitment from French Prime Minister Clément Ader that France would host an acceptable exhibition if he finished the water lily series. Although his health was deteriorating and he was having trouble seeing, Monet set out on this last job with a fresh sense of will.

Just before the renowned artist passed away in 1926, the project was finished. The circular arrangement of the paintings in the room was Monet's deliberate intention for the show; he intended them to surround the spectator completely. Making an immersive experience that would take viewers right inside his water garden was his main objective. A strong visual effect that would connect profoundly with everyone who entered was generated by each canvas, which was painstakingly adapted to match the area. The point of Monet's paintings was to convey the tranquility of the garden, which he had so expertly depicted, by changing the way the observer saw it.

He's enormous canvas paintings are housed in the "Sistine Chapel of Impressionism," a pair of circular chambers in the Orangery of the Jardin des Tuileries in Paris. Seeing these water lily decorations in their permanent location is the greatest way to appreciate Monet's last great work, which depicts an uninterrupted landscape of calm. Tens of thousands of people go to see the works of an 80-year-old genius every time they are on show; his brilliance is awe-inspiring. Without a doubt, Monet is the finest Impressionist of all time.

His capacity to liberate art from the constraints of reality is the key to his legacy. By shifting the focus of painting away from realistic depictions and conventional narratives, Monet allowed light and color to shatter the material world's limits. He came closer to an abstract style of expression in his later works, particularly the water lilies.

Without Monet, the creative scene would have looked quite different since his time, especially from the mid-19th century forward. As a result of his dogged quest of invention, other artists were able to recognize his singular perspective, which stood in sharp contrast to the traditional works shown at France's Royal Academy's yearly displays.

Still, it would be ignoring the bigger picture of creative development. Photography revolutionized how people saw artists, and Monet came to prominence at a crucial juncture, releasing the creative impulses that were vital at the time. The Renaissance, which established many norms for the appreciation and creation of art, may be seen as culminating in this change. For generations of painters to come, Monet's work represented a radical break with conventional wisdom.

Even if many painters of the time didn't see it that way, classic realism was starting to die out during this revolutionary age of painting. Castel-Roc and other realists, along with abstract painters like Kandinsky and Mondrian, continued to work within the framework of developing styles like Cubism, eventually leading to the disintegration of long-established artistic norms.

The way we see color was radically altered by Monet. His work was a departure from the usual since he championed the individuality of the artist rather than conforming to preexisting standards and practices. He said that artists should not try to imitate the viewpoints of others but should instead depend on their own perceptions. Using this outlook, Monet produced works that would go down in art history as landmarks of modernism, characterized by their intensity and brilliance.

The End

Dear reader,

I extend my heartfelt gratitude for acquiring a copy of this work. Your decision to embrace it fills me with immense joy, knowing that I have been able to offer assistance through my words.

In the spirit of sharing joy, I kindly request you to consider leaving a review and spreading the word among others. Your support holds significant meaning to me.

If, by any chance, this piece did not meet your expectations, please accept my sincere apologies.

I assure you that I am committed to improving and striving for excellence in future endeavors. However, above all else, please remember that your act of acquiring this copy demonstrates that you are cherished and loved.

Once again, thank you for your support and for being a part of this journey.

Warm regards

[Leota C. Ray]

www.ingramcontent.com/pod-product-compliance
Lightning Source LLC
Chambersburg PA
CBHW070947220526
45471CB00007B/2921